M000202505

NANTUCKET
The Delaplaine
2021
Long Weekend Guide

No business listed in this guide has provided *anything* free to be included.

Andrew Delaplaine

Senior Editors - ***Renee & Sophie Delaplaine***

Senior Writer - **James Cubby**

Gramercy Park Press
New York London Paris

WANT 3 *FREE* THRILLERS?

Why, of course you do!

If you like these writers--

Vince Flynn, Brad Thor, Tom Clancy, James Patterson, David Baldacci, John Grisham, Brad Meltzer, Daniel Silva, Don DeLillo

If you like these TV series --

House of Cards, Scandal, West Wing, The Good Wife,

You'll love the **unputdownable** series about Jack Houston St. Clair, with political intrigue, romance, and loads of action and suspense.

Madam Secretary, Designated Survivor

Besides writing travel books, I've written political thrillers for many years that have delighted hundreds of thousands of readers. I want to introduce you to my work!
Send me an email and I'll send you a link where you can download the first 3 books in my bestselling series, absolutely FREE.

Mention **this book** when you email me.
andrewdelaplaine@mac.com

NANTUCKET
The Delaplaine
Long Weekend Guide

TABLE OF CONTENTS

Chapter 1
WHY NANTUCKET?

Nantucket was once the "whaling capital of the world," and as such was the place where incredible fortunes were created. You can see some of the stately mansions erected by whaling entrepreneurs of the past, some of which have been converted into inns and B&Bs where you can stay the night, living for a little while in the same surroundings they did.

These days, however, the whalers are lost in the mists of history and legend, replaced by hoards of tourists that descend on the island in the prime summer season.

I always like to go to Nantucket (or places like Cape Cod or the Hamptons) just *before* the season or just *after* it. The weather's just as excellent, the difficulty getting into restaurants nonexistent, the shops and beaches less crowded.

But, you go when you can, of course, and for many, that means summer.

Besides enjoying the old mansions, attractions like the **Whaling Museum**, the cobblestone streets, the cedar shake houses, the romantic restaurants, the harborside pubs where you can share a pint with the locals, you get to take in the areas of the island that remain completely pristine. You get to enjoy the windswept seascapes, cranberry bogs, freshwater ponds, salt marshes.

Nantucket is home to a lot of wealthy people, but you can be right beside them, whether you stay overnight or are just making a day-trip out of it.

As with any tourist town, there are a lot of tourist traps and crappy restaurants, but you'll find good selections here that will not lead you astray.

Chapter 2
GETTING ABOUT

More trips, more ferries,
MORE FUN!

GETTING TO THE ISLAND:

You can get over to Nantucket by air (try Nantucket Air, Cape Air or Jet Blue). Other small regional services operate in the busier summer months.

Or you can travel by ferry:

HY-LINE CRUISES

34 Straight Wharf, Nantucket, 508-228-3949
www.hylinecruises.com
This is a passenger-only cruise line traveling between Nantucket and Hyannis. Moderate rates. Cruises leaving several times daily. Schedule varies by season.

THE STEAMSHIP AUTHORITY
508-477-8600
www.steamshipauthority.com/visitors/nantucket
This is the largest ferry service that travels to the
Islands of Martha's Vineyard and Nantucket from
Cape Cod. Frequent daily departures are offered for
passengers, groups, autos, and trucks. Travel dock to
dock in just an hour. Spacious seating on board with
snack bars, free Wi-Fi and TV. Schedule varies by
season.

GETTING AROUND THE ISLAND

You will not need a car. A lot of people use bikes to
get around, or scooters. Taxis are available, but the
Wave shuttle is all you really need. One negative
about renting a car: parking is a bitch.

THE WAVE
508-228-7025
www.nrtawave.com
The Wave is a **Shuttle Service** operated by the
Nantucket Regional Transit Authority (NRTA). It
takes people all over the island on various routes.

Some routes are served from 10 to 6 while on other routes service runs from 7 a.m. to 11:30 p.m. Tickets are cheap. If you're biking along and get tired, you can hop one of these and load your bike on the racks provided on the shuttle.

Chapter 3
WHERE TO STAY

DID YOU FIND AN INTERESTING PLACE?
If you discover a place you think I should check out
on my next visit, drop me a line, will you? I'll
mention your name if I end up listing it.
andrewdelaplaine@mac.com

21 BROAD HOTEL
21 Broad St, Nantucket, 508-228-4749
www.21broadhotel.com
This chic, Colonial-style hotel features 27 guest
rooms with modern furnishings and luxury perks.
Though the design nods to the typical Nantucket
design elements you find everywhere on the island,
this place is definitely much more modern. Lots of
bright colors, giving the place a very uplifting
atmosphere. You can hang out at their cold-pressed-
juice bar during the day and then gather round the fire
pit at night. It's right near the ferry landing and smack
dab in the middle of the island's restaurant and bar
scene. Amenities: Vitamin C shower, LED Smart TV,
iPod docking station, complimentary Wi-Fi and

breakfast. Hotel features: Back deck with fire pit and spa. Conveniently located 4 minutes from the Steamship Authority ferry terminal.

THE BEACHSIDE AT NANTUCKET
30 North Beach St, Nantucket, 508-228-2241
www.thebeachside.com
This hotel offers 90 air-conditioned rooms and suites including 6 pet-friendly rooms. Amenities include: 26" TVs, DVD player, cable TV, free wireless Internet, free continental breakfast, and DVD library. Facilities include outdoor heated swimming pool, fitness center and free parking. All rooms are non-smoking. Conveniently located close to Nantucket Town and Jetties Beach.

BRASS LANTERN NANTUCKET

11 North Water St, Nantucket, 800-377-6609
www.brasslanternnantucket.com
Located in the Old Historic District, this hotel offers
17 air-conditioned guestrooms and suites. Amenities
include: free Continental breakfast, pet friendly
rooms and canopy beds. Conveniently located just a
short walk from the ferry terminals, the **Whaling
Museum,** local shopping and restaurants.

CENTURY HOUSE

10 Cliff Road, Nantucket, 508 228-0530
www.centuryhouse.com
Built in 1833, this luxury bed and breakfast offers
beautiful renovated guestrooms. A verandah wraps

around the place so there's always a nice place to sit and catch the ubiquitous breezes coming off the water. Amenities include: flat screen TVs, private baths, cable TV, DVD/CD player, book and DVD library, free buffet breakfast, free fresh baked chocolate chip cookies, and free Wi-Fi. Century House offers a beautiful historic location with a wrap-around veranda, patio, and gardens. Conveniently located near local shopping, beaches, and restaurants.

CLIFFSIDE BEACH CLUB
46 Jefferson Ave, Nantucket, 508-228-0618
www.cliffsidebeach.com

This boutique hotel with its own private beach club offers guest 22 charming rooms and suites. Amenities include: free wireless Internet, flat screen TVs, and coffee makers. Rooms are all non-smoking. Facilities include: exercise and spa facility, private bar & café, and pool. Located just one mile from the center of Nantucket's town where guests can enjoy the local shopping and restaurants.

COTTAGES & LOFTS AT THE BOAT BASIN
24 Old South Wharf, Nantucket, 508-325-1499
www.thecottagesnantucket.com
These cottages and lofts offer a unique seaside experience with 24 waterfront cottages and five new deluxe lofts. Guests can enjoy waterfront views, full kitchens and free bicycles. Amenities include: HD Flat screen TVs, air conditioning, free Wi-Fi, free Pre-Arrival concierge service robes and slippers. Pet friendly lodging. Guests receive discounts at sister

hotel restaurants. In-room massages available. Non-smoking property. Free Beach Bus.

GREYDON HOUSE
17 Broad St, Nantucket, 508-228-2468
www.greydonhouse.com
Located in the downtown historic district in an 1850 Greek Revival building and just a 5-minute walk from the ferry, this new boutique hotel offers 18 luxurious guestrooms and suites. Unlike the typical Nantucket design elements, these people have added a lot of modern twists that are very refreshing. Neither the hotel nor the restaurant are priced as low as some of the more "thrifty' Nantucket regulars are used to, but so what? Splurge for once! Amenities: Complimentary mini bar, continental breakfast, toiletries, and flat-screen TV. On-site internationally inspired restaurant has local favorites with an Asian twist (like yuzu-roasted cod fish). Conveniently located just 18 minutes (walking) from the beach and near the Nantucket Whaling Museum, ferry docks and local shopping.

HI-NANTUCKET
Robert B. Johnson Memorial Hostel
31 Western Ave (Surfside), Nantucket, 508-228-0433
http://www.hiusa.org/massachusetts/nantucket/nantuc
ket
Built in a lifesaving station in 1873, this hostel offers single and mixed sex dorms as well as private rooms. Amenities include: free breakfast, free Wi-Fi, parking, game room and guest kitchen. Conveniently located across the street from Surfside Beach. Smoke-

free rooms. Call ahead for co-ed beds. Maximum stay is 7 nights per calendar year.

THE JARED COFFIN HOUSE
29 Broad St, Nantucket, 508-228-2400
www.jaredcoffinhouse.com
The Jared Coffin House, an historic in comprised of the Main House mansion and the Daniel Webster House, offers a variety of comfortable guest rooms with lots of dark woods, printed wallpapers, antiques in the public rooms. Built in 1845 by Jared Coffin, one of the most successful ship owners during the island's prime whaling days, this splendid three-story mansion was constructed in the center of town as his family's residence. It was the first such "mansion" ever built on the New England island.
(Has an excellent in-house restaurant, **Nantucket Prime**, primarily a steakhouse offering prime cuts of dry-aged and wet-aged beef, but it also has excellent fish dishes and a raw bar. There's also a 6-seat Chef's Table offering 2 seatings per night for the chef's 7-course meal.) Amenities include: HD Flat screen

TVs, free parking, free Wi-Fi, computer and printer access, free morning coffee and breakfast pastries, free afternoon coffee and cookies, free bottled water, book and magazine library, and Spa Access at the White Elephant.

NANTUCKET HOTEL & RESORT
77 Easton St, Nantucket, 508-228-4747
www.thenantuckethotel.com
Located 2 blocks from Children's Beach, this grand historic hotel offers a variety of guestrooms, suites, and private cottages. Very good for large parties—they have suites that sleep 11 or 15 persons. Amenities: Complimentary Wi-Fi, flat-screen TVs, private bathrooms, and coffeemakers. Hotel features: 2 seasonal heated pools, a hot tub, fitness center, and a casual restaurant with a year-round deck. Perks include seasonal shuttle service to the ferry and local beaches. Walking distance to beaches, shopping, restaurants, and the harbor.

SUMMER HOUSE COTTAGES
17 Ocean Ave, Nantucket, 508-257-4577
www.thesummerhouse.com
Overlooking the ocean, the Summer House is a boutique collection of inns and restaurants. The hotel features country-style rooms with marble bathrooms, wood floors and vintage furniture. Amenities: Complimentary Wi-Fi (no TVs) and breakfast. Hotel perks: a chic bistro right on the beach, a posh restaurant with patio dining and a piano bar. Freshwater outdoor pool. Complimentary jitney.

THE SUMMER HOUSE INDIA STREET
31 India St, Nantucket, 508-257-4577
www.indiastreetinn.com
The Summer House, located in the same collection as
the Summer House Cottages, offers luxury
accommodations. Guests enjoy staying in the restored
whaling captain's mansion which includes a beautiful
private garden and patio. Amenities: Complimentary
Wi-Fi and breakfast. Private beach and pool access.
Complimentary shuttle and jitney. Conveniently
located near Maria Mitchell Aquarium and Jetties
Beach.

UNION STREET INN
7 Union St, Nantucket, 508-228-9222
www.unioninn.com

This intimate boutique inn offers 12 elegant guestrooms. Amenities include: MALIN+GOETZ bath amenities, flat screen TVs, and free Wi-Fi. Some of the guest rooms feature wood-burning fireplaces. This is the only Nantucket B&B serving a full cooked-to-order breakfast. Afternoon treats include: white chocolate chip cookies with macadamia nuts and carrot cake.

THE WAUWINET INN
120 Wauwinet Rd, Nantucket, 508-228-0145
www.wauwinet.com
Nestled between the Atlantic Ocean and Nantucket Bay, this boutique inn offers charming lodgings with 32 guest rooms and four cottages set across from the Main Inn. The Wauwinet is the only hotel on the island that's a member of Relais & Chateaux. This

place has it all. Amenities include: Plush cotton robes, aroma therapy bath products, HD flat-screen TVs with premium channels, CD/DVD players, free Wi-Fi, free bottled water, free Continental breakfast, free coffee and fresh baked goods for early risers, free fruit anytime, daily newspaper, and DVD library. Non-smoking property.

THE WHITE ELEPHANT
50 Easton St, Nantucket, 508-228-2500
www.whiteelephanthotel.com
An island landmark since the 1920s, this historic hotel offers 67 rooms including guest rooms, suites, garden cottages and in-town lofts. They started off with just a few harbor cottages and have grown over the years to offer a much wider variety of lodgings. At the popular **Brant Point Grill** located here, you

can drink the White Elephant Ale named after this place made by the local **Cisco Brewery** over on Bartlett Park road. Amenities include: free high-speed Wi-Fi, Cable TV, DVD player, HD flat-screen TVs, radio/CD player, bottle water, beach towels, and beach chairs. Most rooms have outdoor patios and decks.

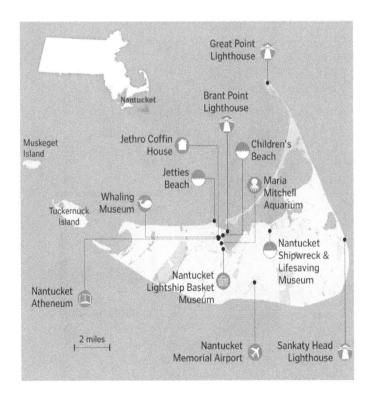

Chapter 4
WHERE TO EAT

DID YOU FIND AN INTERESTING PLACE?
If you discover a place you think I should check out
on my next visit, drop me a line, will you? I'll
mention your name if I end up listing it.
andrewdelaplaine@mac.com

AMERICAN SEASONS

80 Center St, Nantucket, 508-228-7111
www.americanseasons.com
CUISINE: American (New)
DRINKS: Full Bar
SERVING: Dinner
PRICE RANGE: $$$
A little house located in a residential neighborhood, this eatery offers a great selection of American cuisine with a particular focus on regional foods. Favorites: Chicken liver mouse and Baked Salmon. Delicious desserts like Chocolate sorbet. Nice wine selection.

BARTLETT'S FARM

33 Bartlett Farm Rd, Nantucket, 508-228-9403
www.bartlettsfarm.com
CUISINE: Grocery/Sandwiches/Breakfast
DRINKS: No Booze
SERVING: 8 a.m. – 7 p.m.
PRICE RANGE: $$
Grocery that also offers a great selection of sandwiches and prepared entrees and sides. Foods offered include: Bacon Lentil Salad, Pasta Primavera Salad, Tomato Salad, Grilled Organic Chicken Breasts, Rigatoni Marinara, Raw Slaw, and Cous Cous (just to name a few). The homemade chicken salad is excellent. Try their White Chocolate & Raspberry Bread Pudding – so good. Hot lunch specials are offered daily from September through May. Breads are made by a quality supplier here on the island, **Something Natural**, which is also a good

place to stop for sandwiches, by the way.
http://somethingnatural.com/

BLACK-EYED SUSANS
10 India Street, 508-325-0308
www.black-eyedsusans.com
CUISINE: American
DRINKS: No Booze; BYOB; modest corkage fee.
SERVING: Breakfast, Lunch, Dinner
PRICE RANGE: $$ / **cash only**
This little breakfast spot is a favorite of locals and
tourists. Great place for brunch but if you want a
mimosa or bloody Mary make sure to bring your own
booze. For dinner, they have 3 seatings, 6; 7:30 and
10. Indoors or outdoors. Choose one and make a

reservation. (Before, they'd only take reservations for 6, so be sure this doesn't change after we go to press.) Menu favorites include: Curried eggs with broccoli and Thai scrambled eggs for breakfast. For dinner, mustard-soy marinated salmon; local cod "Benedict style," with an egg poached in wine, Niman ranch ham and potatoes; pork scaloppini Marsala. It's really good here. Always busy.

BOARDING HOUSE
12 Federal St, Nantucket, 508-228-9622
www.boardinghousenantucket.com/
CUISINE: American (New)
DRINKS: Full Bar
SERVING: Dinner nightly, Lunch on Sat
PRICE RANGE: $$
Offering a distinctive menu of Mediterranean inspired New American dishes. This eatery, nicknamed BoHo, has earned many accolades, including Best Brunch. Sit out on the patio for the best views. Favorites: Yellow Fin Tuna and Krack Crab stuffed avocado. Popular spot for weekend brunch.

BRANT POINT GRILL
WHITE ELEPHANT HOTEL
50 Easton St, Nantucket, 508-325-1320
www.whiteelephanthotel.com
CUISINE: American
DRINKS: Full Bar
SERVING: Brunch, Lunch, Dinner
PRICE RANGE: $$$$
Located in the White Elephant Hotel, this grill is known to locals as **BPG**. The American menu offers a

variety of fresh seafood, steaks and specialties like the savory lobster dinner. Menu favorites include the Grilled Salmon Salad. Their Sunday Brunch is considered one of the best on the Island. Nice wine selection. (They have a coveted Wine Spectator Award for the excellence of their list.)

BROTHERHOOD OF THIEVES
23 Broad St, Nantucket, 508-228-2551
www.brotherhoodofthieves.com
CUISINE: American
DRINKS: Full bar
SERVING: Lunch, early dinner
PRICE RANGE: $$$
Darkened room gives it a homey feel, both in the bar and restaurant areas. Broiled local codfish; Codfish Parmesan; 12 oz. strip steak; a variety of burgers (for

which they are well known locally); specialty sandwiches like a smokehouse Reuben; the French onion soup is piled high with cheese.

THE CHANTICLEER
9 New St, Siasconset, 508-257-4499
www.chanticleernantucket.com
CUISINE: American (New)
DRINKS: Full Bar
SERVING: Lunch & Dinner
PRICE RANGE: $$$
Upscale dining at its finest in elegant or casual dining rooms. The most charming is the area in the rose garden where you can dine. Menu consists mainly of fish and salads with special dishes like tuna tartar, swordfish and the Maine lobster. Also they have a burger made with a mixture of brisket, short ribs and

sirloin. Fair selection of wine. Book ahead at peak season.

COMPANY OF THE CAULDRON
5 India St, Nantucket, 508-228-4016
www.companyofthecauldron.com
CUISINE: American
DRINKS: Beer & Wine
SERVING: Lunch, early dinner
PRICE RANGE: $$$$
Located in the heart of the Historic District, this small and romantic eatery offers a special fine dining experience with an ever-changing prix fixe menu. Menu favorites include: Herb & Ginger Crusted Rack

of Lamb and Grilled Sliced Flat Iron Steak. Extensive
wine list. Reservations needed.

CRU
1 Straight Wharf, Nantucket, 508-228-9278
www.crunantucket.com
CUISINE: Seafood/American (New)
DRINKS: Full Bar
SERVING: Lunch & Dinner
PRICE RANGE: $$
Stylish eatery located right on the water with a great
seafood selection. This is no beach bum waterfront
hangout. No, it's sophisticated, upscale and charming.
Raw bar. Favorites: Grilled Wester-Ross Salmon and
Haddock Schnitzel. Best lobster roll on the island.
(Well, hmm – OK, *one* of the best.) Crafted cocktails.

DOWNYFLAKE
18 Sparks Ave, Nantucket, 508-228-4533
www.thedownyflake.com

CUISINE: Sandwiches/American
DRINKS: No Booze
SERVING: Breakfast & Lunch
PRICE RANGE: $
Country café (all right, it's a great little dumpy diner) known for their delicious housemade donuts. Great breakfast spot – Smoked salmon and other breakfast treats but don't think of leaving without getting one of their donuts.

DUNE
20 Broad St, Nantucket, 508-228-5550
www.dunenantucket.com
CUISINE: American
DRINKS: Full Bar
SERVING: Dinner
PRICE RANGE: $$$
Created by Michael Getter (a longtime island chef), this restaurant offers an ever-changing creative menu

of traditional American classics. Even though they have 3 rooms for dining, as well as an outdoor patio, plan on booking ahead. It's that good. (And that busy.) Menu favorites include: Sauteed Scottish Salmon and Lemon & Oregano Grilled Chicken. Nice dessert selection but chocolate lovers should try the Chocolate Sampler including: orange chocolate pot de creme, Mexican chocolate torte, coco mousse, and chocolate tiles. Nice wine list.

EASY STREET CANTINA
2 Broad St, Nantucket, 508-228-5418
www.easystreetcantina.com
CUISINE: Mexican-American
DRINKS: No Booze
SERVING: Breakfast & Lunch
PRICE RANGE: $
Right near the ferry, so if you're just arriving, fill up on some inexpensive food before you start touring the island. Has typical breakfast fare (which they serve all day) with some Mexican twists. Lots of New England standard fare like fried shrimp, fried clams, fish & chips, fried scallops—all of it quite good for a super price. Veggie burritos; fish and meat tacos; guacamole; taco salad. Indoor/outdoor seating. You order at the counter.

GALLEY BEACH
54 Jefferson Ave, Nantucket, 508-228-9641
www.galleybeach.net
CUISINE: Seafood
DRINKS: Full Bar

SERVING: Lunch, Dinner; weekend Brunch starts at 10 a.m.
PRICE RANGE: $$$$

Run by the same family since 1958, this restaurant is one of the island's premier restaurants and a favorite marriage location. It's exactly a mile out of town, right on the beach overlooking Nantucket Sound. (Ask anyone. They will point you in the right direction.) One of the more romantic setting on the whole island. In season, they have chairs and table right on the beach. This eatery is elegant yet casual and Chef Neil Ferguson offers a creative seafood menu. Menu favorites include: Lamb Chop with Braised Lamb Neck and Sea Scallops & Lobster; crispy sweetbreads; Atlantic halibut; fluke with braised fennel; roasted guinea fowl. Great sunset views through the wall of windows or at the bar on the beach.

MILLIE'S
326 Madaket Rd, Nantucket, 508-228-8435
www.milliesnantucket.com
CUISINE: Tex-Mex
DRINKS: Full Bar
SERVING: Dinner
PRICE RANGE: $$
On the west end of the island is this place that is the perfect location for a sunset drink. (They have a second floor glassed-in area that gives you a great view.) Chef David Scribner offers a California Baja style menu featuring fresh local seafood, handmade salsa and guacamole, Po Boys and tacos. Menu favorites include: Steak Taco and Scallop Quesadilla. Children's Menu. Bar offers a nice menu of specialty cocktails, champagnes, and wines including some Nantucket labels from places like the **Cisco Brewery**.

THE NAUTILUS
12 Cambridge St, Nantucket, 508-228-0301
www.nautilusnantucket.com
CUISINE: Tapas Bars/American (New) / Asian
fusion
DRINKS: Full Bar
SERVING: Dinner
PRICE RANGE: $$$
Rustic-modern small plates restaurant with a menu
focused on seafood. Favorites: Scallion pancakes,
Oyster tacos and Green curry lobster. Great inventive
craft cocktails like the tasty Barr Hill Gin Marini –
their crown jewel.

ORAN MOR
2 S Beach St, Nantucket, 508-228-8655
www.oranmorbistro.com
CUISINE: American (New)
DRINKS: Full Bar
SERVING: Dinner
PRICE RANGE: $$$
Located in a historic home, this is one of Nantucket's best, offering a creative menu of seasonal dishes, handcrafted cocktails and wines. Menu picks: Duck and Black truffle bucatini. Elegant dining experience.

THE PEARL
12 Federal St, Nantucket, 508-228-9701
www.thepearlnantucket.com
CUISINE: Seafood
DRINKS: Full Bar
SERVING: Dinner
PRICE RANGE: $$$$
Upscale eatery offering a creative Asian Fusion menu. Menu picks: Fried Lobster and Sweet & Sour Halibut. Delicious desserts. Reservations necessary.

THE PROPRIETORS BAR & TABLE
9 India St, Nantucket, 508-228-7477
www.proprietorsnantucket.com
CUISINE: American
DRINKS: Full Bar
SERVING: Dinner
PRICE RANGE: $$$
Chef Tom Berry offers an interesting menu of small and large plate dishes. Menu favorites include: Grass Fed Bavette Steak and Carolina Spatchcock. The wine list offers a curated selection of international bottles from the Old and New World. Interesting desserts for sweet lovers like the Strawberry Mess, a strawberry and cream concoction.

PROVISIONS
3 Harbor Square, Straight Wharf, Nantucket, 508-228-3258
www.provisionsnantucket.com
CUISINE: American
DRINKS: No Booze
SERVING: Lunch, early dinner
PRICE RANGE: $$ / Cash Only
Excellent, reasonably priced sandwich shop on an island known for how expensive everything is. Provisions is famous for its Turkey Terrific Sandwich. I'll tell you why it's so terrific. They cut the turkey real thick and they have a special cranberry sauce that's to die for. But their Caprese Sandwich has to come in second. (Mouthwatering mozzarella and tomatoes.) You order at the counter and they bring your sandwiches to your table. Obviously, they do a lot of take-out here for people just getting off the ferry or just getting on. Great place to pick up a snack for the ferry ride back to the mainland.

SHIP'S INN

13 Fair St, Nantucket, 508-228-0040
www.shipsinnnantucket.com
CUISINE: Bed & Breakfast
DRINKS: Beer & Wine
SERVING: Lunch & Dinner
PRICE RANGE: $$
Bed & Breakfast serving lunch and dinner. Favorites: Halibut in morel sauce and Swordfish. Vegetarian options available. Another thing that'll impress you is the wonderful selection of breads served at beginning of the meal.

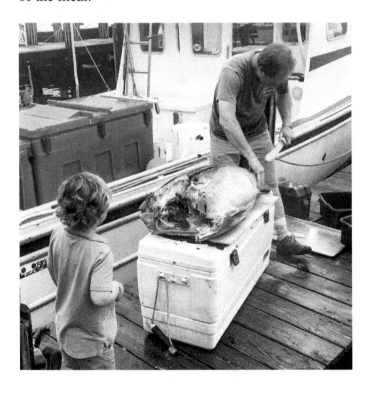

SLIP 14

14 Old S Wharf, Nantucket, 508-228-2033
www.slip14.com
CUISINE: American (New)
DRINKS: Full Bar
SERVING: Lunch & Dinner
PRICE RANGE: $$
Comfortable eatery offering a fish-focused menu.
Favorites: Lobster mac n cheese and Cornmeal
Crusted Calamari. Creative cocktails. Great wine
selection. Water views.

SUMMER HOUSE RESTAURANT

17 Ocean Ave, Siasconset, 508-257-9976
www.thesummerhouse.com
CUISINE: American
DRINKS: Full Bar
SERVING: Breakfast, Lunch, Dinner

PRICE RANGE: $$$

With a beautiful Siasconset location, this eatery from Chef Todd English offers a nice contemporary American menu and impressive wine list. Menu favorites include: char-grilled swordfish; poached lobster salad with green beans; lobster fra diavola. Live piano with sing-alongs. A good alternative to the dining room is their **Beachside Bistro** where you can have lunch under an umbrella and take in the breeze.

TOPPER'S TIDBITS
THE WAUWINET
120 Wauwinet Rd, Nantucket, 508-228-8768
www.wauwinet.com
CUISINE: American
DRINKS: Full bar
SERVING: Breakfast, Lunch, Dinner

PRICE RANGE: $$$

One of the best restaurants on the island, Topper's serves Retsyo Oysters, which are harvested just 300 yards from the Wauwinet. Seasonally inspired menu featuring excellent seafood specialties. (There's a deck where you can get a more casual menu, and the bar always makes a good place to stop by.) Wine Spectator Grand Award for its wine list carrying over 1,500 labels.

VENTUNO
21 Federal St, Nantucket, 508-228-4242
www.ventunorestaurant.com
CUISINE: Italian
DRINKS: Full Bar
SERVING: Dinner

PRICE RANGE: $$$

Located in a Greek revival building, this elegant eatery offers Italian classics with a twist. Try to get a table on the patio outside because they have one of the most appealing on the whole island. Fresh homemade pastas make you think you're in Italy.

Chapter 5
NIGHTLIFE

DID YOU FIND AN INTERESTING PLACE?
If you discover a place you think I should check out
on my next visit, drop me a line, will you? I'll
mention your name if I end up listing it.
andrewdelaplaine@mac.com

CHICKEN BOX
16 Dave St (just off Lower Orange St), Nantucket,
508-228-9717

www.thechickenbox.com
This popular bar is a longtime favorite of locals and tourists. Here you'll find a revolving schedule of live music, pool tables, foosball, darts, and cheap drinks. Outdoor area for smoking and lounging. Cover after 9 p.m. Very busy on weekends and there's usually a line at the door.

CLUB CAR
1 Main St, Nantucket, 508-228-1101
www.theclubcar.com
The Club Car is a railway car transformed into a restaurant and lounge. This place always attracts a crowd with its live music and popular bar scene. Serves lunch and dinner, too.

GALLEY BEACH
54 Jefferson Ave, Nantucket, 508-228-9641
www.galleybeach.net
Though it's primarily a restaurant, a cool crowd of hipsters come together here in the back room in the evenings, making this a great place to go out. Stay

inside or hang out on the sand where they put our comfortable couches and flaming torches provide light. Excellent craft cocktails.

KITTY MURTAUGH'S
4 West Creek Rd, Nantucket, 508-228-0781
www.kittymurtaghs.com
This place offers two levels, and Irish pub upstairs and an intimate dining room downstairs. Decorated with Irish signs and antiques, this place feels like an authentic Irish pub. Upstairs enjoy a mug of Guinness and downstairs enjoy authentic Irish fare.

Chapter 6
WHAT TO SEE & DO

DID YOU FIND AN INTERESTING PLACE?
If you discover a place you think I should check out
on my next visit, drop me a line, will you? I'll
mention your name if I end up listing it.
andrewdelaplaine@mac.com

BRANT POINT MARINE
32 Washington St, Nantucket, 508-228-6244

www.brantpointmarine.com
This is the island's one-stop-shopping for boat sales,
new and used, as well as trailers, hardware, batteries,
repair supplies, electronics equipment, paints,
varnishes, safety equipment, foul weather gear, and
all types of boating wear. Exclusive Island dealer for
Casco Bay Skiffs, Sea Pro, Bristol Skiffs, and Zodiac.
Shellfish Permits are available at the harbormaster's
office next door. You can harvest soft-shell clams on
the mud flats until the middle of June, but quahogs
are good year-round. Get the waders, racks, gloves
and a basket here at Brant Point Marine.

HY-LINE CRUISES
34 Straight Wharf, Nantucket, 508-228-3949
www.hylinecruises.com
This is a passenger-only cruise line traveling between
Nantucket and Hyannis. Moderate rate. Cruises
leaving several times daily. Deep-sea fishing cruises
are also available.

MARIA MITCHELL ASSOCIATION
4 Vestal St, Nantucket, 508-228-9198
www.mariamitchell.org
This is a private non-profit organization founded in 1902 to preserve the legacy of Maria Mitchell, an astronomer, naturalist, librarian and educator. The association operates two observatories, a natural science museum, an aquarium, and the historic birthplace of Maria Mitchell. **BIRD TOURS**: They also offer tours highlighting the island's rich bird population. You get to visit places that are not crowded like **Eel Point**, which you get to either on foot or in a 4-wheel drive vehicle. See if you can spot a sharp-tailed sparrow in the salt marshes. The association offers science and history-related programing. Admission fees at various venues.

NANTUCKET FARMERS & ARTISANS MARKET

Cambridge and North Union Streets, 508-228-3399
www.sustainablenantucket.org
This sustainable Farmers and Artisans Market is at several locations: Downtown on Saturdays and the Muse Parking lot (44 Surfside Road) on Tuesdays from July through August. The 60-odd vendors include growers, artisans, and prepared food purveyors. Get a Flip Flop Quilt from or quilted backpacks from **Island Quilts**. Or a handwoven Alpaca Houndstooth Throw from **Island Weaves**. Or pendants, necklaces, rings and other jewelry from **Keely Smith Designs**. Most of the vendors have stores elsewhere on Nantucket, so if you're not here during the market, you can visit the individual stores. The market also includes live music performances, kids' activities, and demonstrations.

NANTUCKET ISLAND TOURS

Various locations, Nantucket, 508-228-0334
http://www.visit-historic-nantucket.com/nantucket-tours.html
This company offers fully narrated tours of Nantucket Island. The tour, which takes just over an hour, introduces you to the "Little Grey Lady," as Nantucket is known, which was the world's foremost whaling port in the 18th century. The tour includes: The Old Mill, "Sconset" Village, Low Beach, Sankaty Head Lighthouse, Cranberry bogs and Nantucket moors. The tours operate from May through October. Reservations needed.

THE NANTUCKET REGIONAL TRANSIT AUTHORITY
20-R S. Water St, Nantucket, 508-228-7025
www.nrtawave.com
NRTA offers island wide shuttle and van service.
Island wide service includes nine routes with 13
buses.

NANTUCKET SHIPWRECK & LIFESAVING MUSEUM
158 Polpis Rd, Nantucket, 508-228-1885
www.nantucketshipwreck.org
This museum celebrates the memory of the islanders
who risked their lives to save shipwrecked mariners
like the Massachusetts Humane Society, United
States Life-Saving Service and the United States
Coast Guard. There are over 700 documented wrecks

in the difficult waters surrounding Nantucket, and this is the place to relive some of that history. A special treat here is some eerie film footage of the Italian liner "Andrea Doria" as she lists to her side after being struck broadside in a fogbank off Nantucket by the Swedish liner "Stockholm." The museum features revolving exhibitions, films, family-friendly programs and special events. Nominal fee.

THE OLD MILL
50 Prospect Street, Nantucket, 508-228-1894
www.nha.org/sites/oldmill.html#_=_
Built in 1746 by Nathan Wilbur,
This "Old Mill" is the oldest functioning mill in the U.S. At one time there were four "smock mills" that overlooked Nantucket town however this is the only remaining mill. Nominal fee. Tour available.

PETER FOULGER MUSEUM
15 Broad St, Nantucket, 508-228-1655
www.nha.org
This museum exhibits paintings, furniture, and other
items illustrating the island's rich history. Nominal
fee.

THE QUAKER MEETINGHOUSE
7 Fair St, Nantucket, 508-228-1894
www.nha.org/sites/quakermeetinghouse.html
This site celebrates the early days of the Quakers in
the years after 1708. This meetinghouse was erected
in 1832 and originally served as a school for the
Wilburite Sect. In the 1940s the Quakers began
meeting here again. This was the first museum of the
Nantucket Historical Association. Nominal fee. Tours
available.

SHEARWATER EXCURSIONS
Straight Wharf, Nantucket, 508-228-7037
www.explorenantucket.com
This is a family-run, year-round eco-tour company
that offers tours of the many ecosystems in the
Nantucket area and also the underdeveloped outer
islands of Tuckernuck and Muskeget. These
excursions provide a great educational adventure with
narration. Two ferry lines run between Hyannis and
Nantucket several times daily during the summer.
Moderate fee for six-hour excursion.

SHELLFISHING
See **Brant Point Marine** for details.

THE STEAMSHIP AUTHORITY

508- 477-8600

www.steamshipauthority.com

This is the largest ferry service that travels to the Islands of Martha's Vineyard and Nantucket from Cape Cod. Frequent daily departures are offered for passengers, groups, autos, and trucks. Travel dock to dock in just an hour. Spacious seating on board with snack bars, free Wi-Fi and TV.

TRIPLE EIGHT DISTILLERY
CISCO BREWERS
NANTUCKET VINEYARD

5 Bartlett Farm Road, Nantucket, 508-325-5929

www.ciscobrewers.com

This operation has evolved from a winery initially to include a brewery as well as a distillery where they make spirits. The tours are especially interesting.

WHALING MUSEUM

13 Broad St, Nantucket, 508-228-1894
www.nha.org

This museum primarily exhibits its large collection of whaling artifacts and memorabilia. The centerpiece of the museum's collection is a complete skeleton of a 45-foot bull whale that is suspended from the ceiling. Other highlights include an 1849 Fresnel lens used in the **Sankaty Head Lighthouse** and workings of the 1881 town clock. There's a big collection of artifacts from the doomed ship "Essex," which was struck (and sunk) by a sperm whale it was chasing. (Sounds like the plot of "Moby Dick," doesn't it? It ought to. That real-life story inspired Herman Melville to write the book, which I find impossible to read.) The building housing the museum was a candle factory a century ago. Nominal admission fee. Nantucket Historical Association located on the second level.

Chapter 7
SHOPPING & SERVICES

DID YOU FIND AN INTERESTING PLACE?
If you discover a place you think I should check out
on my next visit, drop me a line, will you? I'll
mention your name if I end up listing it.
andrewdelaplaine@mac.com

CHRISTOPHER WHEAT

585-329-8997

www.christopherwheat.com

Wheat paints all sorts of island scenes and is highly regarded in these parts for his work.

ERICA WILSON

NANTUCKET SAILBAG TOTES

ERICA WILSON

25 Main St, Nantucket, 508-228-9881

www.ericawilson.com

Hip boutique offering women's and children's fashions. Also available are bracelets, accent jewelry, needlework canvases and supplies.

HENLEY & SLOANE

18A Federal St, Nantucket, 508-228-6209

www.henleyandsloane.com

Men's clothing featuring the finest traditional English shirt makers and clothiers. Flawless designs and tailoring. They are justly famous for their striped socks. Make sure you get a couple of pairs.

JACK WILLS
11 South Water St, Nantucket, 508-332-1601
www.jackwills.com
Jack Wills is a middle-tier British clothing brand aimed at university students. Jack Wills has 80 stores around the globe. (This was the first on in America.) Colorful polo shirts, cable knit sweaters, totes, a little bit of everything. As preppy as Ralph Lauren (and a little more genuine).

MILLY & GRACE
2 Washington St, Nantucket, 508-901-5051
www.millyandgrace.com
Set in a little ivy covered building, this shop offers feminine and vintage inspired fashions and home

décor. Here you'll find everything from flirty dresses to cashmere, jewelry and beautiful home décor. The shop was named after the owners' grandmothers.

MITCHELL'S BOOK CORNER
54 Main St, Nantucket, 508-228-1080
www.mitchellsbookcorner.com
This is a full service, independent bookstore that's been here for over 40 years boasting an extensive selection of books numbering in the thousands about Nantucket, whaling, history of the island, and a stock of titles in all genres. Has lots of readings by visiting authors, other activities.

MURRAY'S TOGGERY SHOP
62 Main St, Nantucket, 508-228-0437
www.nantucketreds.com
This store stocks a variety of clothing and gifts from around the world including: Nantucket Red's Pants, shorts, shirts, and jewelry. Brands carried include: Bill's Khakis, Castaway Clothing, Diane Reilly Jewelry, Eliza B, Hatley, La Soula, Lacoste,

Leatherman, New England Nauticals, Peter Millar, Smathers & Branson, and Southern Tide.

NANTUCKET BOOKWORKS
25 Broad Street, Nantucket, 508-228-4000
www.nantucketbookpartners.com
This funky little bookshop is stocked with great books, toys, gifts, cards and local music. An excellent place to stop in to browse the hundreds of books about Nantucket. Nice lavish coffeetable books, too. The owner says her bestseller is Nathaniel Philbrick's book from 2000, "In the Heart of the Sea," which recounts the tragedy of the "Essex," a whaling ship struck and sunk by a sperm whale in 1820 in the South Pacific. you can see some artifacts in the **Whaling Museum**.

NANTUCKET LOOMS
51 Main St, Nantucket, 508-228-1908
www.nantucketlooms.com

Known the world over since they opened in 1968 for their textiles, hand-woven throws and beautiful one-of-a-kind mohair and cashmere creations. Women love this place. Home furnishings and accessories. Interior design services available.

SUNKEN SHIP
12 Broad St, Nantucket, 508-228-9226
www.sunkenship.com
Retail shop offering huge selection of t-shirts, hats, sweatshirts, souvenirs, and almost anything you're looking for. Also available: scuba lessons, tank fills, diving equipment, and dive charters. It's been here since 1975 and the island wouldn't be the same without it.

SUSTAINABLE NANTUCKET'S FARMERS & ARTISANS MARKET

Various locations

www.sustainablenantucket.org

Farmers & Artisans market features a vast selection from local growers, food producers, and artisans. Great place to begin the day with breakfast before lunging into the wide variety of offerings here. Go to Wicked Island Bakery for coffee and one of their mouthwatering breakfast buns:

http://wickedislandbakery.com/

You'll find everything including: organically grown seasonal produce, honey, handmade Italian cheeses, jewelry, photography, glass art, t-shirts, soap, and flowers. Live music, kids' activity tables and demonstrations. Check website for location.

YOUNG'S BICYCLE SHOP
6 Broad St, Nantucket, 508-228-1151
www.youngsbicycleshop.com
This is your one-stop-shopping destination for bikes
and bike gear. They sell, rent, and service bikes. They
also offer car and jeep rentals.

<u>INDEX</u>

WANT 3 **FREE** THRILLERS?

Why, of course you do!

If you like these writers--

Vince Flynn, Brad Thor, Tom Clancy, James Patterson, David Baldacci, John Grisham, Brad Meltzer, Daniel Silva, Don DeLillo

If you like these TV series --

House of Cards, Scandal, West Wing, The Good Wife,

You'll love the **unputdownable** series about
Jack Houston St. Clair, with political intrigue, romance,
and loads of action and suspense.

Madam Secretary, Designated Survivor

Besides writing travel books, I've written political thrillers for many years that have delighted hundreds of thousands of readers. I want to introduce you to my work!
Send me an email and I'll send you a link where you can download the first 3 books in my bestselling series, absolutely FREE.

Mention **this book** when you email me.

andrewdelaplaine@mac.com

CPSIA information can be obtained
at www.ICGtesting.com
Printed in the USA
LVHW020522110721
692282LV00011B/1035